A - Z
of
GRAMMAR

A teacher's survival guide for the primary curriculum

Full coverage of terminology
Simple explanations with examples

Published by Keen Kite Books
An imprint of HarperCollinsPublishers Ltd
1 London Bridge Street
London SE1 9GF

ISBN 9780008172923

First published in 2016

10 9 8 7 6 5 4 3 2 1

Text and design © 2016 Keen Kite Books, an imprint of HarperCollinsPublishers Ltd

Commissioning Editor: Michelle I'Anson
Inside Concept Design: Paul Oates
Project Managers: Sonia Dawkins and Shelley Teasdale
Cover Design: Anthony Godber
Text Design and Layout: Q2A Media
Production: Lyndsey Rogers
Printed in Great Britain by Martins the Printers

A CIP record of this book is available from the British Library.

Images are ©Steve Evans

Abstract nouns

An abstract noun names something that does not physically exist and so cannot be touched. The names of qualities and characteristics, emotions and feelings, concepts and ideas are abstract nouns.

happiness   **beauty**   **imagination**

Active voice

There are two different ways of presenting the same information in a sentence using verbs. These are the active voice and the passive voice. In the active voice, the subject of the sentence does the action:

Nina is feeding the rabbit.
  | |
subject   verb

The cat chased a mouse.
  | |
subject verb

In the passive voice, the subject of the sentence has the action done to it:

The rabbit is being fed by Nina.
  | |
subject   verb

The mouse was chased by a cat.
  | |
subject   verb

The passive voice uses the verb **to be** with the past participle of the verb:

is being fed   **was chased**

It usually sounds more natural to use the active voice when writing, but sometimes it is better to use the passive voice if there is uncertainty about who did something, or to avoid assigning blame, or if a formal tone is required.

The bus shelter has been vandalised.

The front door has been left open again.

A study was carried out to establish how much traffic passes the school.

A B C D E F G H I J K L M N O P Q R S T U V W X Y Z

Adjective phrases

An adjective phrase contains at least one adjective. It can also contain other word classes, for example, adverbs.

a **brown** bear

a **big brown** bear

a **big scary brown** bear

a **really huge** bear

Adjectives

An adjective is a word that modifies a noun; adjectives make nouns more specific. They do this in a number of ways:

how nouns feel or what they are like:

a **happy** child

a **strange** boy

a **joyful** occasion

what they look like:

a **large** tree

a **spotty** dress

a **gorgeous** beach

what they sound, smell, taste or feel like:

a **noisy** party

a **stinky** cheese

a **delicious** cake

a **hard** seat

what colour they are:

a **yellow** bag

dark hair

green leaves

where they come from:

our **German** relatives

my **American** friend

a **northern** accent

what something is made from:

chocolate cake

a **wooden** box

a **velvet** scarf

Adjectives can also be used after the verb **be**, as its complement:

The box was **wooden**

I am **happy**

Teachers are **patient**

Comparative adjectives and superlative adjectives

When making comparisons between people or things, a comparative or superlative adjective is required. In the examples below, **taller** is the comparative form of **tall** and **tallest** is the superlative.

Rory is <u>tall</u>.

Rory is <u>taller</u> than his brother.

Rory is the <u>tallest</u> boy in his class.

See page 11 for more about comparative adjectives and page 38 for more about superlative adjectives.

Good and bad

The adjectives **good** and **bad** don't follow the normal rules for comparative and superlative forms.

good	better	best
bad	worse	worst

Adverb phrases

An adverb phrase is a phrase containing at least one adverb, which acts in the same way as an adverb.

Katie tiptoed <u>very quietly</u> across the room.

The man shouted 'Fire!' <u>as loudly as possible</u>.

She danced <u>really gracefully</u>.

Adverbials

Adverbials

An adverbial can be an adverb, an adverb phrase, a preposition phrase or a subordinate clause. It describes how the action in the sentence is happening, for example when it is happening, where it is happening, how it is happening, how often it is happening or why it is happening. Not all sentences have adverbials.

> **Suddenly**, it started to rain **heavily**.

> **Breathing quietly**, Lee crept out of the room.

> You probably won't notice it **after a while**.

> I'll make a cup of tea **when I've finished reading this**.

An adverbial can go anywhere in a sentence:

> I **greatly** admire your courage.   The door closed **with a loud bang**.

> **Honestly**, I didn't mean to be rude to you.

When the adverbial is at the start of the sentence it is called a fronted adverbial. These are usually followed by a comma:

> **Seriously**, are you wearing that?

> **At the end of the match**, the players shook hands.

> **Bitterly disappointed**, the home supporters left the stadium quickly.

> **When the cake is golden brown**, take it out of the oven.

Adverbs

Adverbs perform many different functions. They give additional information relating to when, how often, where, how, how much and possibility. They can also act as cohesive devices, making links between sentences or paragraphs. Many adverbs end in the suffix –*ly*, but not all of them do, and not every word that ends in –*ly* is an adverb.

They can modify verbs:

When and how often:

> I arrived <u>late</u>.   She is going <u>tomorrow</u>.   You <u>never</u> play with me.

Where:

> We live <u>here</u>.   The plane flew <u>south</u>.   Parminder looked <u>up</u>.

How (or how much):

> Ella runs <u>fast</u>.   The children sang <u>loudly</u>.   I <u>really</u> want to see that film.

Adverbs can also modify other word classes:

other adverbs:	*adjectives:*	*nouns:*	*pronouns:*
They waited <u>very</u> anxiously.	The dog was <u>certainly</u> fierce.	It was <u>quite</u> an occasion.	<u>Nearly</u> everyone attended.

prepositions:

> Go over <u>there</u>!

Adverbs can also modify whole clauses:

> <u>Fortunately</u> it didn't rain.   <u>Maybe</u> we can go next week.

> <u>Perhaps</u> it will happen soon.

Adverbs can act as cohesive devices, linking sentences or paragraphs. This kind of adverb is often, but not always, a compound. It is important to note that you can only link main clauses with an adverb (adverbs cannot introduce subordinate clauses), so an adverb cannot follow a comma but must be either in a new sentence or follow a semi-colon.

> More traffic will result in increased noise. <u>Furthermore</u>, there may be danger to pedestrians.

> My mother seemed very angry; <u>however</u>, I knew she was really scared.

Antonyms

An antonym is a word opposite in meaning to another. For example, **forget** is the antonym of **remember**.

Antonyms can be used to show a contrast:

> William had hoped by now to be <u>rich</u>; he was shocked to realise he was actually rather <u>poor</u>.

> After so many years her <u>love</u> had turned to <u>hate</u>.

Using an antonym with a negative can add emphasis to something that might seem surprising:

> Maria was <u>not unhappy</u> that the party had been cancelled.
> (Maria was actually happy about it)

> This government policy is <u>not unpopular</u> with the public.
> (The policy is actually popular)

Articles (*also see* Determiners)

The word **the** is called the definite article.
The word **a** is called the indefinite article.
If the word after **a** begins with a vowel, **an** is used instead.

Auxiliary verbs

There are three verbs that can be used as auxiliary verbs: **to be**, **to have** and **to do**. These can be combined with other verbs to make different tenses. **To be**, **to have** and **to do** can also be used as main verbs.

> I <u>was</u> washing my hair.   The chicken <u>had</u> crossed the road.

> <u>Did</u> you tidy your room?

Be, **have** and **do** are irregular verbs, which means that they do not follow the usual rules for making verb forms.

Be

As a main verb:

I **am** happy.

You **are** sad.

She **is** tired.

They **are** late.

He **was** scared.

You **were** angry.

As an auxiliary verb:

I **am** running.

You **are** jumping.

She is **brushing** her hair.

They **are** going out.

You **were** dancing.

He **was** bouncing.

Have

As a main verb:

I **have** a cat.

You **have** a dog.

She **has** a rabbit.

We **have** a parrot.

They **have** no pets.

We **had** some grapes

As an auxiliary verb:

I **have** danced.

He **had** got confused.

You **had** lost your keys.

I **had** been feeling ill.

We **have** been shopping.

She **has** broken her leg.

Do

As a main verb:

I **do** well at sport.

You **do** badly at some subjects.

She **does** anything sporty.

We **do** something active at the weekends.

We **did** well today.

As an auxiliary verb:

I **do** not like her.

You **do** enjoy running.

She **does** love chocolate.

We **did** tidy up our rooms.

They **do** practise hard.

You **did** like him.

Clauses

A clause is a group of words which contains a subject and a verb. There are two types of clauses: Main clauses (detailed on page 21) and Subordinate clauses (detailed on page 34).

Collective nouns

A collective noun is a group or collection of things:

pack

bunch

flock

Depending on whether we are thinking of the group as an impersonal unit or as a collection of individuals, collective nouns can be used with either a singular or plural verb.

Command

This is a sentence that gives orders or instructions. The verb used for commands is called 'the imperative' and is usually found at the start of the sentence. It can end with a full stop or, if extra importance needs to be emphasised, an exclamation mark:

Give me the paper.

Come over here.

Stop right there!

When giving a polite command, the verb might not be at the start of the sentence:

Please stop talking.

Common nouns

These nouns are used to name every example of a certain type of thing. They start with a lower case letter:

girl

city

picture

There are three different types of common nouns: Concrete nouns (detailed on page 12), Abstract nouns (detailed on page 3) and Collective nouns (detailed above).

Comparative adjectives

The comparative shows that a person or thing has more of a certain quality than another person or thing. To make the comparative form of an adjective, add the suffix **-er** to the end.

> dull + -er = duller   green + -er = greener   clever + -er = cleverer

However, not all comparatives are made in this way. If the adjective is quite a long word, **more** is used instead.

> beautiful → more beautiful   eccentric → more eccentric

> interesting → more interesting

Complement

A complement is a word or phrase that tells us something about the subject of the sentence. It is a noun, a noun phrase, an adjective, an adjective phrase, a pronoun or a subordinate clause. The verbs **be**, **become**, **feel** and **seem** are the most common verbs to use this construction.

> Laura is <u>an architect</u>.

> They became <u>very good friends</u> when they worked together.

> The boys felt <u>silly</u> when they had to dress up.

> She seems <u>perfectly happy</u>.

Complex sentences *or* Multi-clause sentences

A complex sentence has a main clause and one or more subordinate clauses:

> Zoya threw the ball to Marion, who was standing on the other side of the pitch.

> Today is my birthday, although my party isn't until tomorrow, which is a pity.

A
B
C
D
E
F
G
H
I
J
K
L
M
N
O
P
Q
R
S
T
U
V
W
X
Y
Z

Compound sentences *or* Multi-clause sentences

A compound sentence contains two or more main clauses joined by a co-ordinating conjunction:

> Zoya threw the ball and Marion caught it.

> Today is my birthday but my party is tomorrow.

Compound words

A compound word is one that is created from two or more root words. Many English words are produced in this way.

> girl + friend = girlfriend

> soft + ware = software

> after + shave = aftershave

Compound words can be written in different ways:

- **as one word:**   bookcase   wallpaper   outrun   skateboard
- **as two words:**   post office   fire engine   eye shadow   Roman Catholic
- **with a hyphen:**   bone-dry   one-way   face-lift   middle-of-the-road

Concrete nouns

A concrete noun is a physical object that can actually be touched:

> donkey   bicycle   doughnut

Conjunctions

A conjunction is a word that is used to link two words, two phrases or two clauses:

> **I will need to save up some money <u>before</u> I can buy a new phone.**
> (**before** shows time relationship)

> **Please let me know <u>when</u> you want to go home.**
> (**when** shows time relationship)

There are two main types of conjunction: Co-ordinating conjunctions (detailed below) and Subordinating conjunctions (detailed on page 35).

Contractions

A contraction is a word created by joining two words together. To do this, one or more letters need to be removed. An apostrophe is used to show where the letter or letters have been taken out:

> **do not → don't**   **it is → it's**   **I have → I've**

Contractions are used when speaking and in informal writing, such as emails to friends.

Co-ordinating conjunctions

A co-ordinating conjunction links two things that are as important as each other, such as two words, two phrases or two main clauses. The most common are **and**, **or** and **but**:

> **I love fish <u>and</u> chips.**

> **You can have a biscuit <u>or</u> a cake.**

> **It was raining <u>but</u> we had our coats.**

It can also show a contrast between two things:

> **Joe is having a birthday party <u>but</u> he hasn't invited me.**

A
B
C
D
E
F
G
H
I
J
K
L
M
N
O
P
Q
R
S
T
U
V
W
X
Y
Z

Determiners

Determiners

A determiner is a word that precedes a noun and serves to introduce and add context to the noun. There are different kinds of determiners:

Articles

The word **the** is called the definite article:

> the robot   the traffic   the footballers

The word **a** is called the indefinite article:

> a caravan   a giraffe   a scooter

If the word after **a** begins with a vowel, **an** is used instead:

> an animal   an umbrella   an orange pencil

Other determiners

Other types of determiners give different information about the noun:

- the distance between the speaker and the thing they are talking about:

> <u>this</u> shoe   <u>these</u> books   <u>that</u> man   <u>those</u> houses

- who owns the thing:

> <u>my</u> bag   <u>your</u> phone   <u>his</u> kite   <u>her</u> mug

> <u>its</u> door   <u>our</u> car   <u>their</u> garden

- how much or how many:

> <u>some</u> sugar   <u>much</u> money   <u>both</u> girls

> <u>few</u> people   <u>many</u> adults   <u>several</u> birds

- the exact number:

> <u>one</u> melon   the <u>two</u> brothers   <u>fifty</u> roses   <u>ten thousand</u> years

- how something is shared out:

Every child got a prize.

Each runner is given a number.

Either team could win on the day.

Neither side is playing well at the moment.

Direct speech

This involves quoting exactly what a person says. For direct speech, use inverted commas and verbs like **say**, **reply**, **answer**, **mutter** and **shout**. When relaying a conversation, start a new paragraph every time a different person speaks.

> "Hello Sarah," said Mike. "What are you doing here?"
>
> "I'm meeting my friends here," she replied. "We are having lunch and then we are going to the cinema to see the new *Hunger Games* film."
>
> "Who's going?" asked Mike.
>
> Sarah said, "Lucy, Aila, Rachel and Fiona."

Double negatives

A negative is a word like **not**, **nor**, **never** or **nothing**, which means **no**. When two of these are used in a sentence it is known as a double negative. This should not be used in standard English, though it can be a feature of some dialects:

I did**n't** have any money.
(NOT I did**n't** have **no** money.)

We have **never** been there.
(NOT We have**n't** **never** been there.)

He did**n't** do anything wrong.
(NOT He did**n't** do **nothing** wrong.)

A B C D E F G H I J K L M N O P Q R S T U V W X Y Z

Ellipsis

Ellipsis is omitting a word or phrase which is expected and predictable.

> Do you like jazz? I don't like it.
> > Do you like jazz? I don't.

> Julie looked behind and she started to run.
> > Julie looked behind and started to run.

An ellipsis is also the term for a punctuation mark. This is depicted by a sequence of three dots indicating an omission in text.

Exclamation

This is a sentence which expresses a strong feeling. It ends with an exclamation mark:

> What a laugh!

> You're here at last!

> I never want to see you again!

Formal language

This is the type of language that should be used in official or serious environments such as in the classroom.

Dear Mrs Jenkins

I am sorry I missed your telephone call yesterday. I was out with two of my friends, Jack and Anna. We were at an attraction called Lazergame, where you chase and shoot each other with lasers. It was really good fun and I am hoping to go again soon.

I will see you at five o'clock on Friday, assuming your train is on time.

Yours sincerely,

Eve

Some of the features of formal language:

- full forms (**I am**, **you are**, **I will**)
- use of punctuation (**I**, **Lazergame**, **Jack**, **Anna**)
- no slang (**sorry** not **soz**)
- longer, more complex sentences
- formal opening and closing (**Dear**, **Yours sincerely**)
- more difficult words (**attraction**, **assuming**)
- not using symbols instead of words.

Formal and informal vocabulary

Informal and slang words should be avoided in written work, unless writing a conversation. For example, use:

child (not **kid**)   **man** (not **guy**)   **friend** (not **pal**)

satisfactory (not **OK**)   **angry** (not **ballistic**)   **wealthy** (not **minted**)

relax (not **chill**)   **impressive** (not **awesome**)

very good (not **well good**)

Another feature of formal language is the Subjunctive (detailed on page 34).

Future tense

The future tense is used if an action is still to happen. This is done by using **will** or **shall** and then the verb:

I <u>will be</u> there on time.   He says he <u>will phone</u> later today.

We <u>shall see</u> if that's true.

The future tense can also be made using **go**:

He <u>is going to</u> sing tomorrow.

English has no distinct future tense.

A
B
C
D
E
F
G
H
I
J
K
L
M
N
O
P
Q
R
S
T
U
V
W
X
Y
Z

A
B
C
D
E
F
G
H
I
J
K
L
M
N
O
P
Q
R
S
T
U
V
W
X
Y
Z

I and me

Avoid confusing **I** and **me**. Use **I** for the subject of the sentence, and **me** for the object.

> **Helen and I are going swimming.**
> (NOT **Helen and me are going swimming.**)

> **Kevin threw the water balloon at Linda and me.**
> (NOT **Kevin threw the water balloon at Linda and I.**)

If unsure whether to use **I** or **me** in a sentence like this, take the other person out of the sentence and see if it still makes sense:

> **Helen and I are going swimming.**
> **> I am going swimming. (NOT Me is going swimming.)**

> **Kevin threw the water balloon at Linda and me.**
> **> Kevin threw the water balloon at me. (NOT Kevin threw the water balloon at I.)**

Indirect speech

This relays what a person has said but does not quote it exactly. No inverted commas, question marks or exclamation marks are used in indirect speech.

> **Mike asked Sarah what she was doing in the cafe. She told him she was meeting her friends for lunch and then going to the cinema. Mike asked who was going and Sarah told him it was Lucy, Aila, Rachel and Fiona.**

Informal language

This is the relaxed type of language used to write to friends or close family, for example in emails or texts:

> Hey how R U? Soz i missed ur call. @ lazergame with jack n anna.
> It was beast! cant wait 2 go again. I'll phone u l8r. ☺

Some features of informal language:

- slang words (**beast**)
- contracted forms (**I'll**)
- abbreviations (**R U, soz, ur, n**)
- smileys or emoticons (☺)
- lack of punctuation (**jack, anna, cant, i**)
- informal greeting (**Hey**)
- short simple sentences
- simple vocabulary
- numbers or symbols (**2** for **to**, **@** for **at** or **l8r** for **later**).

A
B
C
D
E
F
G
H
I
J
K
L
M
N
O
P
Q
R
S
T
U
V
W
X
Y
Z

Layout

The arrangement of text on a page is important and a good layout improves clarity and ease of use. As well as dividing text into paragraphs, there are a number of other elements that can be introduced to enhance readability.

Headings

A heading is a title or caption that appears at the top of the page and summarises the topic of the text below. It often appears in bold and in a larger type size than the main text.

Subheadings

If text needs to be split into sections, the title given to each of these is a subheading. Subheadings are often bold or underlined.

Columns

Lists of information can appear in vertical columns of text, each with a heading.

Bullet points

Lists can also be shown with bullet points which have a centred dot before each entry.

Here's an example of good layout:

Emblems of the United States of America

Background

Each of the 50 states that make up the United States of America has three emblems to represent it. These are a bird, a flower and a tree.

History

The first state flower was selected in 1892 when Washington chose the coast rhododendron as its emblem. Texas was the first to select a state tree – the pecan – in 1919. In 1927, seven states chose the birds that they wanted as their emblems.

State	State Bird	State Tree	State Flower
Alabama	yellowhammer	longleaf pine	camellia
Alaska	willow ptarmigan	sitka spruce	forget-me-not
Arizona	cactus wren	blue palo verde	saguaro cactus blossom

Other US territories with state emblems:

- Guam
- Northern Marianas

Main clauses

A main clause is the essential component of a sentence and would make sense if it stood on its own. Every sentence has a main clause:

<u>Matthew ate a cake</u> which was covered in chocolate.

After looking carefully in both directions, <u>Ali crossed the road</u>.

Modal verbs

The modal verbs are **can**, **could**, **may**, **might**, **must**, **shall**, **should**, **will**, **would** and **ought (to)**. They are used with other verbs to indicate certain meanings like possibility, doubt or obligation. Unlike all other verbs, they do not change their form:

I <u>can</u> ride a bike.

Olivia <u>can</u> speak Italian.

My friends <u>can</u> all come to my party.

I <u>could</u> be late so don't wait for me.

You <u>may</u> be right.

I <u>might</u> go to the library after school.

You <u>must</u> listen to the teacher.

<u>Shall</u> we take the dog for a walk?

You <u>should</u> clean your teeth at least twice a day.

<u>Will</u> you hang your jacket up?

I <u>would</u> love a cup of tea.

We <u>ought</u> to leave now.

Non-standard English

Non-standard English is the language that is often spoken but does not always follow the rules of grammar. This should be avoided in written work, unless you are writing very informally, or, for example, writing a conversation between people who don't use Standard English.

Noun phrases

A phrase containing at least one noun is called a noun phrase:

a tall <u>girl</u>

an extremely tall <u>girl</u>

an extremely tall <u>girl</u> with piercing blue eyes

Nouns

A noun is a word that names something. In a sentence, the nouns are the words that identify which people, places or things are involved.

There are different kinds of nouns: Common nouns (detailed on page 10), Proper nouns (detailed on page 30), Singular nouns (detailed on page 33) and Plural nouns (detailed on page 25).

Object

The object is the person or thing that has the action of the verb done to it. It is a noun, a noun phrase or a pronoun. It comes after the verb. Not all sentences have an object.

Kim loves <u>chocolate</u>.

I have lost <u>my new green rucksack</u>.

Are you going to ask <u>him</u> to the prom?

Paragraphs

Every paragraph starts on a new line. A paragraph details one idea or one part of an argument. A new paragraph is started when discussing the next idea or another part of an argument:

> **More British households have dogs than any other pets. A survey has found that 25% of homes in the UK have a dog. The labrador retriever remains the most popular dog, followed by the cocker spaniel and springer spaniel.**
>
> **Cats are the next most popular pet in the country, being found in 19% of British homes. The favourite breed by far is the shorthair domesticated cat, although the Siamese, Burmese and Persian are all increasing in popularity.**

When quoting direct speech, a new paragraph is started for each new speaker:

> **"Are you playing in the match after school today?" asked Nathan.**
>
> **"No," replied Simon. "I have to go to the dentist."**

Within story writing, each new event in the story should have its own paragraph. These paragraphs, however, benefit from being linked in order to add cohesion to the narrative.

Passive voice (*also see* Active voice)

In the passive voice, the subject of the sentence has the action done to it:

> **The rabbit is being fed by Nina.**
>
>   *subject   verb*

> **The mouse was chased by a cat.**
>
>   *subject   verb*

The passive voice uses the verb **to be** with the past participle of the verb:

> **is being fed**   **was chased**

It is better to use the passive voice if there is uncertainty about who did something, or to avoid assigning blame, or if a formal tone is required.

> **The front door has been left open again.**

> **A study was carried out to establish how much traffic passes the school.**

Past tense

If an action has already happened, use the past tense. There are four types of past tense:

Simple past tense

For most verbs, add **-ed** to the end to make the simple past tense. Add **-d** if the verb already ends in **e**:

> The dog <u>barked</u> at the postman.   I <u>scrambled</u> over the wall.

Progressive past tense

This is also known as the continuous past tense. Add **-ing** to the verb and put it after **was** or **were**. This is used to talk about something that was still happening at a certain point in the past or when something else happened:

> That was the summer when Jack and I <u>were learning</u> to ride.

> Richard <u>was cooking</u> dinner when the fire alarm went off.

Present perfect tense

This uses **has** or **have** with the simple past tense of the verb. The present perfect tense is used to show that an action has been completed:

> Abby <u>has finished</u> her project on Japan.   I <u>have baked</u> a cake for the party.

Past perfect tense

This uses **had** with the simple past tense of the verb. This is used to show that something had been completed when something else happened:

> Matthew <u>had finished</u> his lunch before the others had even started.

> I <u>had packed</u> my suitcase when the taxi arrived.

Personal pronouns

A personal pronoun is used instead of the subject or object of a sentence:

> <u>She</u> is good at maths.   Nobody likes <u>him</u>.

Phrases

A phrase is a sequence of words which form a concept. Phrases do not contain verbs.

> **a busy street**   **the family pet**   **very good at tennis**

Although a phrase makes sense, it is not a full sentence and requires more words to make it complete:

> **We live on a busy street.**   **The family pet is a tortoise called Bob.**

Plural nouns

The plural form of a noun is used to mean more than one of a thing:

> **two pictures**   **ten elephants**   **four schools**

Possessive case

The possessive (or possessive case) is used to demonstrate ownership. Add **'s** to the end of the noun that is the owner:

> **my mother's sister**   **Nick's football boots**

If the noun is a plural that already ends in **s**, put an apostrophe at the end of the word:

> **the soldiers' uniforms**   **those boys' bicycles**

Don't use **'s** to make a plural noun. It is only used for showing the possessive.

Some nouns are plural but do not end in **s**, for example 'children'. Treat these nouns as if they were singular:

> **the children's coats**

Some singular nouns end in **s**. In this case you add an apostrophe and an **s**:

> **the Princess's crown**

Names that end in **s**, like James, can be written either:

> **James's hat**   **James' hat**

A B C D E F G H I J K L M N O P Q R S T U V W X Y Z

Possessive pronouns

A possessive pronoun is used to demonstrate that something belongs to a person or thing:

> We had to move out when <u>our</u> house was flooded.

> I think the blue jacket is <u>mine</u>.

> The dog buried <u>its</u> bone in the garden.

Prefixes

A prefix is a letter or group of letters that is added to the beginning of a word to make a new word. Adding a prefix to a word changes the word's meaning:

> un- + usual = unusual

> un- + cover = uncover

> un- + happiness = unhappiness

The prefix **un-** means 'not' so when adding it to a word, the new word has the opposite meaning to the original:

> un- + friendly = unfriendly (not friendly)

Other prefixes that do this are **dis-**, **non-** and **in-**:

> dis- + agree = disagree   non- + fiction = nonfiction   in- + expensive = inexpensive

When adding **in-** before words that begin with certain letters, the **n** changes:

- before **l**, **in-** changes to **il-**:   il- + legal = illegal

- before **m**, **in-** changes to **im-**:   im- + modest = immodest

- before **p**, **in-** changes to **im-**:   im- + patient = impatient

- before **r**, **in-** changes to **ir-**:   ir- + rational = irrational

Other prefixes that are useful to know are:

prefix	meaning	example	language it comes from
anti-	against	anticlockwise	Greek
pro-	in favour of	prowar	Latin
de-	undo or remove	defrost	Latin
bi-	two or twice	bimonthly	Latin
auto-	self	autobiography	Greek
ante-	before	antenatal	Latin
co-	together	cooperate	Latin
pre-	before	predate	Latin
re-	again	reheat	Latin
circum-	round or about	circumference	Latin
ex-	out or outside of	external	Latin
inter-	between	international	Latin
mis-	wrong or false	misbehave	Old English
sub-	under	subway	Latin
super-	larger, over or beyond	superpower	Latin
mini-	small	miniskirt	English
over-	too much	overeat	English
trans-	across	transmit	Latin
tele-	distant	television	Greek
ultra-	extremely	ultramodern	Latin
micro-	small	microcomputer	Greek
tri-	three	tricycle	Latin

Preposition phrases

A preposition phrase acts as an adjective or an adverbial in a sentence. It contains a preposition followed by a noun, a noun phrase or a pronoun.

> She shut the dogs <u>in the kitchen</u>. ├— adverbial

> A plastic bag was floating <u>in the wind</u>. ├— adverbial

> The book <u>on the bathroom floor</u> was wet. ├— adjectival

Prepositions

A preposition is a word that is used before a noun or a pronoun, to convey how things are related or connected to each other. For example, prepositions can describe:

- where a person or thing is:

> a cat <u>in</u> the garden   a book <u>on</u> the table   a sock <u>under</u> the bed

Other prepositions like this include:

> above   beside   underneath   near   below

- the movement of something or someone:

> The train came <u>into</u> the station.   We pushed <u>through</u> the crowd.

Other prepositions like this include:

> around   down   up   onto   to

They also show how things are related in time:

> I haven't seen my auntie <u>since</u> last week.

Present tense

If the action is happening now, the present tense is used. There are two types of present tense that can be applied:

Simple present tense

This uses the verb as it is, or has an additional **-s** at the end:

> I <u>like</u> broccoli.   You <u>love</u> peas.   Max <u>hates</u> carrots.

> We <u>enjoy</u> swimming.   Martin and Kate <u>play</u> the piano.

Progressive present tense

This is also known as the continuous present tense. For this tense, add the ending **-ing** to the verb and put a form of the verb **be** in front of it:

> I <u>am doing</u> my homework.

> You <u>are annoying</u> me.

> Lara <u>is painting</u> a picture.

Pronouns

A pronoun is a word that is used in place of a noun. A pronoun is used instead of repeating the name of a person, place or thing:

> **Rachel lives next door to me. Rachel is in my class.**
> **> Rachel lives next door to me. <u>She</u> is in my class.**

> **That is the book I am reading just now. The book is very funny.**
> **> That is the book I am reading just now. <u>It</u> is very funny.**

> **I like to sit in the garden. The garden is very sunny.**
> **> I like to sit in the garden. <u>It</u> is very sunny.**

A
B
C
D
E
F
G
H
I
J
K
L
M
N
O
P
Q
R
S
T
U
V
W
X
Y
Z

A pronoun can be used to link different parts of text:

> **The runners are ready to go. <u>They</u> are waiting for the starting pistol.**
> (**They** links with **the runners**)

> **I don't like my maths teacher. <u>He</u> shouts a lot.**
> (**He** links with **my maths teacher**)

Proper nouns

These nouns are used to identify a particular person, place or thing. They start with a capital letter:

> **Andy Murray**   **Switzerland**   **River Seine**

Question

This is a sentence which asks for information. It begins with a questioning word like **what**, **who**, **which**, **where**, **when**, **how** or **why**. It can also begin with a verb. It ends with a question mark:

> **What is your name?**   **Have you seen my keys?**

> **Where is Mount Everest?**

Question tags

A question tag is a short question at the end of a statement. They are used to check that the listener agrees with the speaker. They are common in speech and informal writing but should not be used in formal writing:

> **You've cleaned your room, <u>haven't you</u>?**

> **We're not going to that, <u>are we</u>?**

Relative clauses

A relative clause is a type of subordinate clause. It begins with a relative pronoun: **who**, **whom**, **whose**, **which** or **that**:

> Robbie has a cat <u>who likes fish</u>.

> David has one brother, <u>whose name is Peter</u>.

> Our teacher is off sick today, <u>which is unusual for her</u>.

Relative clauses are often 'dropped in' to the middle of a sentence:

> My teacher, whose name is Mo Green, is fantastic.

Relative pronouns are described in more detail below.

A relative clause can be used without the relative pronoun **that** or **which**:

> She has lost the book <u>that</u> I lent her.   She has lost the book I lent her.

> That is the car <u>which</u> he has just bought.   That is the car he has just bought.

Relative pronouns

Two different parts of a sentence can be linked using a relative pronoun instead of a noun. The relative pronouns are **who**, **whom**, **whose**, **which** and **that**. They introduce information about a noun in an earlier part of the sentence. This noun is known as the antecedent. Use **who**, **whom** and **whose** when the antecedent is a person, and **which** and **that** when it is not a person.

who: Use **who** when the antecedent is the subject of the second clause:

> I have an aunt <u>who</u> lives in Australia.

A
B
C
D
E
F
G
H
I
J
K
L
M
N
O
P
Q
R
S
T
U
V
W
X
Y
Z

whom: Use **whom** when the antecedent is the object of the second clause:

> It was the same man <u>whom</u> we had seen earlier.

whose: Use **whose** to show that something belongs to the antecedent:

> Scott has a brother <u>whose</u> name is Jamie.

which: Use **which** when the antecedent is not a person:

> We took the road <u>which</u> leads to the sea.

that: Use **that** when the antecedent is not a person:

> George brought the sandwiches <u>that</u> he had made the night before.

Root words

A root word is a word that can stand alone and still make sense, for example **read**. Prefixes and suffixes can be added to a root word in order to create new words:

> read   reads   reading   reader   readable   misread   reread

Sentences

A sentence is a group of words that expresses an idea or conveys a situation. A sentence must have:

- a capital letter at the beginning of the first word
- a full stop, a question mark or an exclamation mark at the end
- a finite verb.

Simple sentences *or* Single-clause sentences

A simple sentence contains just one main clause:

> **Zoya threw the ball.**   **Today is my birthday.**

Singular nouns

The singular form of a noun is used to mean only one of a thing:

> **a picture**   **one elephant**   **the school**

Standard English

Standard English is the form of English most easily recognised as a major world language. It can be spoken in any accent. Standard English can be used formally or informally but should always be used in formal situations.

Statement

This is a sentence which relays something. A statement usually starts with the subject of the sentence. It ends with a full stop:

> **Berlin is the capital of Germany.**

> **I am going home now.**   **It's raining.**

A B C D E F G H I J K L M N O P Q R S T U V W X Y Z

Subject

The subject is the person or thing that does the action in a sentence. It is a noun, a noun phrase or a pronoun. It comes before the verb.

Louise fell asleep.

Dogs don't like fireworks.

She threw a cushion across the room.

In a sentence using the passive voice, the subject is the person or thing having the action done to it.

The sandwich was eaten.

Subjunctive

The subjunctive is a feature of formal language. This is a form of verb that is sometimes used to show the possibility of something happening or the wish for it to happen. Use **were** instead of **was**:

If your father **were** here he would help you.

If I **were** rich I would buy a house like that.

Susan has always wished she **were** taller.

I wouldn't do that if I **were** you.

Subordinate clauses

A subordinate clause is less important than the main clause. It would not make sense if it stood on its own because it is not a full sentence. It gives more information about the main clause:

When he had looked carefully in both directions, Ali crossed the road.

Matthew enjoyed the cake **because it was covered in chocolate**.

Subordinate clauses often start with **when**, **if**, **because** or **that**. A Relative clause is a type of subordinate clause (detailed on page 31).

A B C D E F G H I J K L M N O P Q R S T U V W X Y Z

Subordinating conjunctions

A subordinating conjunction introduces a subordinate clause:

The teacher was angry <u>because</u> the pupils would not pay attention.

Mark read his book <u>while</u> he waited for his mum to arrive.

I must tell you some exciting news <u>before</u> we get started.

Some dogs go a bit crazy <u>when</u> it's windy.

Suffixes

A suffix is a letter or group of letters that is added to the end of a word to make a new word. Adding a suffix to a word changes a word's meaning:

sad + -ness = sadness

Two useful suffixes are **-ful** and **-less**. These are added to words to make adjectives. The suffix **-ful** means 'full of', while **-less** means 'without':

hope + -ful = hopeful (full of hope)

hope + -less = hopeless (without hope)

pain + -ful = painful (full of pain)

pain + -less = painless (without pain)

A B C D E F G H I J K L M N O P Q R S T U V W X Y Z

Here are some other suffixes that make adjectives:

suffix	meaning	example
-able	able to	readable
-al	related to	traditional
-ary	related to	revolutionary
-ible	able to	reversible
-ic	related to	rhythmic
-ish	fairly or rather	smallish
-ist	prejudiced	racist
-ive	tending to	divisive
-like	resembling	dreamlike
-ous	full of	perilous
-y	like or full of	grassy

There are some suffixes that mean 'the state of', 'the condition of' or 'the quality of'. These form nouns:

suffix	example
-ness	blind + -ness = blindness
-ity	stupid + -ity = stupidity
-ance	accept + -ance = acceptance
-ation	examine + -ation = examination
-dom	bore + -dom = boredom
-ence	depend + -ence = dependence
-hood	child + -hood = childhood
-ion	elect + -ion = election
-ship	member + -ship = membership

Other suffixes that make nouns include:

suffix	meaning	example
-er	person who does something	painter
-er	thing that does something	fastener
-er	person from a place	islander
-ant	person who does something	defendant
-ism	action or condition	criticism
-ism	prejudice	sexism
-ment	state of having	employment
-ology	study of	biology

Suffixes that make verbs include:

suffix	meaning	example
-ate	become or take on	hyphenate
-ise or -ize	change or affect	motorise
-ify	make or become	purify
-en	make or become	dampen

Often an adverb can be made from an adjective by adding the suffix **-ly**, which means 'in this way':

proper + -ly = properly

real + -ly = really

week + -ly = weekly

Superlative adjectives

The superlative shows that a person or thing has the most of a certain quality out of a group of people or things.

To make the superlative form of an adjective, add the suffix **-est** to the end.

dull + -est = dullest

green + -est = greenest

clever + -est = cleverest

If the adjective is quite a long word, use **most** to make the superlative.

beautiful → most beautiful

eccentric → most eccentric

interesting → most interesting

Synonyms

To avoid repetition and introduce variety in writing, it helps to use synonyms of overused words. A synonym is a word that means the same, or nearly the same as another word.

Here are some words to avoid repeating and some possible synonyms to try instead:

- nice:

attractive   charming   agreeable   delightful

pleasant   likeable   pleasurable

- great:

  excellent   outstanding   superb

  skilful   first-rate   tremendous

- look:

  glance   peek   gaze   stare   watch

  survey   examine   study   gape

- big:

  gigantic   immense   massive

  vast   enormous   colossal

Beware that a word that is a synonym for one meaning of a word might not work for another. Replacing **good** with **well-behaved** in the phrase 'a good child' works fine, but **well-behaved** does not work instead of **good** in 'a good book'.

Tense

The tense of a verb specifies when the action takes place.

Tense agreement

It is important not to mix up tenses when writing. If starting off in the past tense, keep to the past tense throughout.

> I was walking down the street when I <u>saw</u> my friend coming towards me.
> (NOT I was walking down the street when I <u>see</u> my friend coming towards me.)

Verb phrases • Verbs

Verb phrases

A verb phrase contains an auxiliary verb and sometimes an adverb:

> I <u>am enjoying</u> the summer holiday.

> He <u>had been learning</u> to play the piano.

> She <u>is always complaining</u> about her teachers.

Verbs (*also see* Modal verbs)

A verb is a word that describes an action or a state of being. Every sentence must contain a verb or a verb phrase:

> We always <u>listen</u> to the radio in the car.

> Andrew <u>is</u> a Scout.

> The man <u>walks</u> slowly up the hill.

> Jessica <u>fainted</u>.

> Adam <u>is having</u> a haircut.

> People <u>have lived</u> in this place for hundreds of years.

Verb contractions

Some shortened forms of verbs are used in non-standard English. These should not be used in writing:

- **ain't = am not, are not, is not**

  > He <u>is not</u> here yet.
  > (NOT He <u>ain't</u> here yet.)

- **shouldnt've = should not have**

  > You <u>should not have</u> done that.
  > (NOT You <u>shouldnt've</u> done that.)

- **innit = is it not?**

  > That is great, <u>is it not</u>?
  > (NOT That is great, <u>innit</u>?)

Verb inflections

In Standard English, the correct verb form must be used for the past tense of irregular verbs. Some verbs (irregular verbs) have two different forms for the past tense, for example **see**. These are called the past tense and the past participle. The past tense is the one that makes the simple past of the verb. The past participle is the one used with **have**.

I <u>saw</u> = the past tense

I have <u>seen</u> = the past participle

I <u>saw</u> him yesterday. (NOT I <u>seen</u> him yesterday.)

You should have <u>gone</u> to bed earlier. (NOT You should have <u>went</u> to bed earlier.)

He <u>did</u> his homework in school. (NOT He <u>done</u> his homework in school.)

Also, write **I was sitting** not **I was sat**:

I was <u>sitting</u> on the wall when Zain appeared.
(NOT I was <u>sat</u> on the wall when Zain appeared.)

Subject and verb agreement

In Standard English, the correct form of the verb must be used for the subject of the sentence.

He <u>was</u> asleep when the fire broke out.
(NOT He <u>were</u> asleep when the fire broke out.)

We <u>were</u> happy to hear the news. (NOT We <u>was</u> happy to hear the news.)

Word class

Every word in a language can be classified into a group according to what it does within a sentence. These groups are known as word classes. Some words can belong to multiple word classes, depending on how they are used in a sentence.

Word families

A word family is a group of words that are related to each other because they originate from the same root word:

sign   signature   signage   signify   significant   signpost   signal
undersign   design   designate

solve   solver   solvent   soluble   solution   dissolve   resolve

Index

A

Abstract nouns 3
Active voice 3
Adjective phrases **4**, 11
Adjectives **4**, 7, 11, 28, 35, 36, 38
   Adjective phrases **4**, 11
   Comparative adjectives 5, **11**
   Superlative adjectives 5, **38**
Adverb phrases **5**, 6, 11
Adverbials **6**, 28
Adverbs 5, 6, **7**, 37, 40
Antecedent 31–32
Antonyms 8
Apostrophes 13, 25
Articles **8**, 14
Auxiliary verbs **8–9**, 40

B

Bullet points 20

C

Clauses **10**, 13, 31, 33
   Main clauses 7, 11, 12, 13, **21**, 34
   Relative clauses **31**, 34
   Subordinate clauses 6, 7, 11, 31, **34**, 35
Collective nouns 10
Columns 20
Command 10
Common nouns 10
Comparative adjectives 5, **11**
Complement 11
Complex sentences 11
Compound sentences 12
Compound words 12
Concrete nouns 12
Conjunctions **13**, 35
Contractions **13**, 40
Co-ordinating conjunctions 12, **13**

D

Definite article 14
Determiners 14–15
Direct speech **15**, 23
Double negatives 15

E

Ellipsis 16
Exclamation 10, **16**, 18, 33

F

Formal language **16–17**, 30, 34
Fronted adverbial 6
Future tense 17

H

Headings 20

I

I and me 18
Indefinite article 14
Indirect speech 18
Informal language 13, **19**, 22, 30
Irregular verbs – past tense 41

L

Layout 20

M

Main clauses 7, 11, 12, 13, **21**, 34
Me and I 18
Modal verbs 21
Multi-clause sentences 11, 12

N

Negatives 15
Non-standard English **22**, 40
Noun phrases **22**, 28, 34
Nouns 4, 7, 11, 14, **22**, 25, 28, 29, 31, 34, 36–37
   Abstract nouns 3
   Collective nouns 10
   Common nouns 10
   Concrete nouns 12
   Noun phrases **22**, 28, 34
   Plural nouns 25
   Proper nouns 30
   Singular nouns 33

O

Object 18, **22**, 24, 32

P

Paragraphs 15, 20, **23**
Passive voice 23
Past perfect tense 24
Past tense **24**, 39, 41
Perfect present tense 24
Personal pronouns 24
Phrases 13, **25**
   Adjective phrases 4, 11
   Adverb phrases **5**, 6, 11
   Noun phrases **22**, 28, 34
   Preposition phrases 28
   Verb phrases 40
Plural nouns 25
Possessive case 25
Possessive pronouns 26
Prefixes **26–27**, 32
Preposition phrases 28
Prepositions 28
Present perfect tense 24
Present tense 29
Progressive past tense 24

Progressive present tense 29
Pronouns 7, 11, 22, 28, **29–30**, 31, 34
   Personal pronouns 24
   Possessive pronouns 26
   Relative pronouns 31
Proper nouns 30

Q

Question 30
Question tags 30

R

Relative clauses **31**, 34
Relative pronouns **31**
Root words 12, **32**, 42

S

Sentences 25, 28, 30, 31, **33**, 34
   Complex sentences 11, 17
   Compound sentences 12
   Multi-clause sentences 11, 12
   Simple sentences 33
Simple past tense 24
Simple present tense 29
Simple sentences 33
Single-clause sentences 33
Singular nouns 33
Standard English 15, **33**, 41
Statement 30, **33**
Subheadings 20
Subject 3, 10, 11, 18, 23, 24, 31, 33, **34**, 41
Subject and verb agreement 41
Subjunctive 34
Subordinate clauses 6, 7, 11, 31, **34**, 35
Subordinating conjunctions 35
Suffixes 7, 11, 32, **35–37**, 38
Superlative adjectives 5, **38**
Synonyms 38

Index

T

Tense 39
  Future tense 17
  Past perfect tense 24
  Past tense **24**, 39, 41
  Perfect present tense 24
  Present tense 29
  Progressive past tense 24
  Progressive present tense 29
  Simple past tense 24
  Simple present tense 29
Tense agreement 39

V

Verb contractions 40
Verb inflections 41
Verb phrases 40
Verbs 8, 10, 11, 15, 17, 22, 23, 24, 25,
29, 30, 33, 34, 37, **40–41**
  Auxiliary verbs **8–9**, 40
  Modal verbs 21

W

Word class 42
Word families 42